INTRODUCTION

THE CHANGING FACE OF THE URBAN SCENE

Open to change but always retaining a smattering of Nordic cool, Stockholm is an edgy, flirtatious, party city. The early noughties trend of sleek, white minimalism may have highlighted the captal as a pilgrim site for the design-conscious, but today the city has achieved a maturity that challenges the notion that Stockholm and its inhabitants are 'only' ravishingly beautiful. Even the smart, conservative, groomed central area of Östermalm has opened itself up to cosmopolitan influences. And Södermalm – the island south of Gamla Stan (the Old Town) – has established itself as the young, trendy, boho-chic area with a cultural and commercial value that deserves more than a passing nod.

As well as this shift in focus away from the centre, the city has also altered stylistically. The ubiquitous white tabletops, clean seating areas and tealight ambience has been updated and many commercial interiors have taken on individual, experimental and altogether more fun undertones. The locals themselves, with their well-spoken English, zest for life and love of travelling, have recently taken all these foreign influences to heart. Yet amid all their enthusiasm is a strong sense of self-awareness. Stockholmers have an incredible quality of never taking things too far. Whether it's in design, architecture, fashion or catering, Swedes just seem to achieve the ideal balance. They've even got the perfect word for it, *lagom*, which means 'just right'.

ESSENTIAL INFO

FACTS, FIGURES AND USEFUL ADDRESSES

TOURIST OFFICE
Vasagatan 14
T 5082 8508
www.visitstockholm.com

TRANSPORT
Car hire
Avis
T 07 7082 0082
Hertz
T 07 7121 1212
Metro
T 600 1000
www.sl.se/english
Taxis
Taxi Kurir
T 300 000
Taxi Stockholm
T 150 000
Taxi 020
T 020 202 020
Taxis can be hailed in the street

EMERGENCY SERVICES
Ambulance (and general emergencies)
T 112
Police (non-emergency)
T 114 14
24-hour pharmacy
Apotek CW Scheele
Klarabergsgatan 64
T 07 7145 0450

EMBASSIES
British Embassy
Skarpögatan 6-8
T 671 3000
www.britishembassy.se
US Embassy
Dag Hammarskjölds Väg 31
T 783 5300
stockholm.usembassy.gov

POSTAL SERVICES
Post Office
Centralstationen
T 781 2425
Shipping
UPS
T 020 788 799
www.ups.com

BOOKS
City of My Dreams by Per Andrews
Fogelstrom (Penfield Press)
The Girl with the Dragon Tattoo
by Stieg Larsson (Quercus Books)

WEBSITES
Architecture
www.arkitekturmuseet.se
Art
www.modernamuseet.se
Design
www.svenskform.se
Newspaper
www.thelocal.se

EVENTS
Market
www.market-art.se
Stockholm Furniture Fair
www.stockholmfurniturefair.se

COST OF LIVING
Taxi from Arlanda Airport to city centre
SEK495
Cappuccino
SEK25
Packet of cigarettes
SEK50
Daily newspaper
SEK10
Bottle of champagne
SEK250

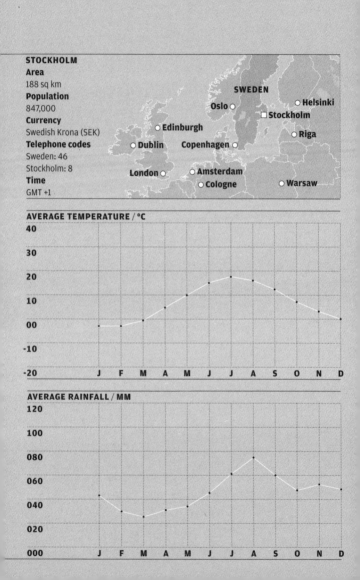

STOCKHOLM
Area
188 sq km
Population
847,000
Currency
Swedish Krona (SEK)
Telephone codes
Sweden: 46
Stockholm: 8
Time
GMT +1

SWEDEN

Oslo ○   ○ Helsinki
□ Stockholm
○ Edinburgh
○ Riga
○ Dublin   Copenhagen ○

London ○   ○ Amsterdam
○ Cologne   ○ Warsaw

AVERAGE TEMPERATURE / °C

40											
30											
20											
10											
00											
-10											
-20	J	F	M	A	M	J	J	A	S	O	N	D

AVERAGE RAINFALL / MM

120											
100											
080											
060											
040											
020											
000	J	F	M	A	M	J	J	A	S	O	N	D

NEIGHBOURHOODS

THE AREAS YOU NEED TO KNOW AND WHY

To help you navigate the city, we've chosen the most interesting districts (see below and the map inside the back cover) and colour-coded our featured venues, according to their location; those venues that are outside these areas are not coloured.

ÖSTERMALM

With the most prime property in Sweden, manicured boulevards and chic shopping centres, this is the place to check out which labels are in and which are 'so last year'. Filled with yummy mummys, the snazzy media set and plenty of old money, its happy residents rarely go anywhere else.

SKEPPSHOLMEN

Otherwise known as Museum Island, this tiny area was once heavily littered with military buildings; today it is to all intents and purposes made up of Svensk Form (Svensksundsvägen 13, T 463 31 30), Arkitekturmuseet (T 5872 7000) and Moderna Museet (see p010). All three are worthy of a visit.

NORRMALM

The bustling city centre Norrmalm is the capital's business hub. Filled with offices, coffee chains and lunch spots, it's not exactly a quaint area, but when it contains Stockholm's largest department store, NK – think the equivalent of Selfridges or Bloomingdales – then who needs cute?

SÖDERMALM

Until ten years ago parts were considered too dangerous to venture into at night (in Swedish terms anyway) but today this trendy, boho part of town tells a different story. Transformed into a creative hub, the area is rich in cutting-edge boutiques, yoga studios and beatnik cafés.

VASASTADEN

This mainly residential district attracts families looking for a bit more space but still wanting the benefits of inner-city life. A few more bars and restaurants have sprung up recently to give the place an increasingly hip vibe, but for the most part it is local eateries and organic delis.

GAMLA STAN

Packed full of character and tourists, the Old Town is the olde worlde part of the city. A maze of cobbled streets and terracotta-coloured buildings, the area is pretty much made up of restaurants, bars and gift shops. Veer away from the main strip, Västerlanggatan, to find some charming antique shops and adorable cafés.

KUNGSHOLMEN

Up-and-coming as a residential area for young creatives who have been pushed out of Östermalm by rocketing rents. The island's huge houses have been converted into loft-living spaces with a few cosy local bistros and small galleries springing up on these otherwise deserted streets.

DJURGÅRDEN

This lush, green, urban garden is the city's oasis. The area contains the zoo, funfair and several museums, and manages to do so in the least tacky way possible. The path along the water, shaded by the trees, is definitely up there with the best jogging routes in the world.

LANDMARKS

THE SHAPE OF THE CITY SKYLINE

Alongside the regular collection of painted canvases and framed photographs that line the walls of the Moderna Museet (overleaf) are rectangular windows that reveal breathtaking views of Stockholm's harbour. In other words, for the Swedes, a view over the landscape is just as beautiful as any work of art.

Then again, given that the city is built on 14 islands and a series of 24,000 smaller ones in the archipelago beyond, it isn't that surprising that it casts a striking picture. Separated only by a short walk across one of 57 bridges, each of the main islands has its own character. Norrmalm has a buzzing, city-centre feel, while Gamla Stan, just a stop away on the subway, is all picturesque cobbled streets and cosy cafés. Östermalm, which is a densely filled residential and shopping area, is very different from lush, green Djurgården, but lies just a quick skip over Djurgårdsbron.

With the skyline so dominated by the water, landmarks tend to take second place. Kaknästornet (see p012), the telecom building, can be seen from almost anywhere. Newer structures, such as Ericsson Globe (see p093), which was completed in 1989, and the Moderna Museet, rebuilt between 1995 and 1998, fit very comfortably within Stockholm's panorama, while Kulturhuset (see p015) in Norrmalm, located slap bang in the city centre, is perhaps the ideal landmark from which to navigate.

For full addresses, see Resources.

Moderna Museet

Originally housed in a 19th-century navy drill house, it wasn't until the mid-1990s that the Museum of Modern Art had its striking minimal makeover. Designed by Spanish architect Rafael Moneo in collaboration with White Architects, the museum was forced to close for two years due to problems with damp, but emerged triumphant in 2004 with an improved interior and an extended permanent collection. Now it stands proud on Skeppsholmen, as loved for its art – the museum houses one of the largest collections of 20th-century works in Europe, plus numerous Swedish and Nordic sculptures, paintings and installations – as its spacious galleries, subtle exterior and outstanding café. *Skeppsholmen, T 5195 5289, www.modernamuseet.se*

Kaknästornet

Known as the central 'spider' in the web of Sweden's TV and radio networks, this imposing 155m-high steel and concrete structure has little other connection to an arachnid. Drawn up by architects Bengt Lindroos and Hans Borgström, it took four years to build and opened in 1967. Like so many other 1960s buildings, the stark tower has dramatically divided city opinion over the years. Few residents, however, could argue that the view from the top-floor restaurant (which, despite a refurb, doesn't quite make the grade in terms of dining) is anything but spectacular. *Mörka Kroken 28-30, T 667 2105, www.kaknastornet.se*

Wenner-Gren Centre
Designed by Sune Lindström and Alf Bydén, and completed in 1962, the 74m high-rise is one of the tallest buildings in the whole of Sweden. The centre is named after the late Axel Wenner-Gren, a businessman who donated the funds for the project. It is composed of two main structures: the Helicon, the lower, semi-circular building surrounding the tower that provides housing for visiting scientists, and the tower, the Pylon, which is home to the Wenner-Gren Foundation, an organisation dedicated to the support of international scientific exchange.
Sveavägen 166, T 736 9800,
www.swgc.org

Koppartälten

Built in 1787 by set designer Louis-Jean Desprez for the King's Guardsmen, the three Copper Tents are a magical addition to the already dreamlike Haga Park. Gustav III commissioned the tents as part of an attempt to build his own version of Versailles, which had apparently made a great impact on him. Unfortunately, the tents are all that remain of his vision as the project was terminated by his assassination in 1792. Today, the middle tent houses a museum detailing the park's history, while the chic café located in the eastern tent, designed by Torbjörn Olsson, is an aluminium masterpiece.

Hagaparken, Solna, T 277 002,
www.koppartalten.se

Kulturhuset

A counterpoint to the commercialism of the inner-city redevelopment of Hötorget, Peter Celsing's remarkable building at Sergels Torg beat off all other contenders in a 1965 competition. Incorporating two buildings into one – the Kulturhuset (Culture House) and Civic Theatre with the Riksbanken (Bank of Sweden) – was no simple task. Rather than try to unify two such different functions, Celsing did just the opposite. Kulturhuset was given a completely glass-fronted façade that showcases the activities inside, while in stark contrast the Bank is a heavy, introverted, black granite cube.
Sergels Torg 7, T 5083 1508,
www.kulturhuset.stockholm.se

HOTELS

WHERE TO STAY AND WHICH ROOMS TO BOOK

A few years ago, Stockholm would have struggled to house the visitors to any large event or conference. This is no longer so, thanks to several new hotels having opened recently – the mighty Clarion Sign (see p029), with 558 rooms, and the smaller 201-room Hotel Nobis (opposite). While both have been well received, older hotels have not fallen out of favour, and impeccable service and constant updates have kept the established names on top.

The Grand Hôtel (see p028), which renovated its lobby and opened a new bar and restaurant on the ground floor, gained 76 new rooms and suites when it acquired the Burmanska Palace next door in 2006, and in 2011 37 additional rooms were updated. The Berns Hotel (see p020) has given its Clock Suite an overhaul and is renovating the rest. While none of the city's newly built hotels could be described as monolithic – save perhaps the Clarion (Ringvägen 98, T 462 1000) – the boutique concept has until recently been largely unrepresented. However, two trendy newcomers to the boutique formula are the bohemian Story Hotel (see p024) and the fashionable Lydmar (see p030), whose bar alone is worth a visit. For traditional, Hotel Esplanade (see p021) is perhaps the only centrally located qualifier, but for real cosiness you need to go out of town, where the Gåshaga (see p018) has just 13 modern rooms with sea views that are unsurpassed.

For full addresses and room rates, see Resources.

Hotel Nobis

Opened in 2010, this is probably the most sophisticated luxury hotel in town. Local design trio Claesson Koivisto Rune have combined earthy colours, oak, Carrara marble and leather to create a space that doesn't make too much of a fuss about itself. The Golden Bar is a favourite for after-work drinks among locals, while the downstairs restaurant Caina (T 614 1030) offers excellent Italian food; gastronomic director Stefano Catenacci is also chef de cuisine at Operakällaren (see p045). Some of the rooms, such as Room 467 (above) overlook Berzelii Park, and the opulent Nobis Suite features original 1800s wood-panelled walls and a green-tiled fireplace. For a simpler but equally elegant stay, ask for one of the round tower rooms.
Norrmalmstorg 2-4, T 614 1000, www.nobishotel.com

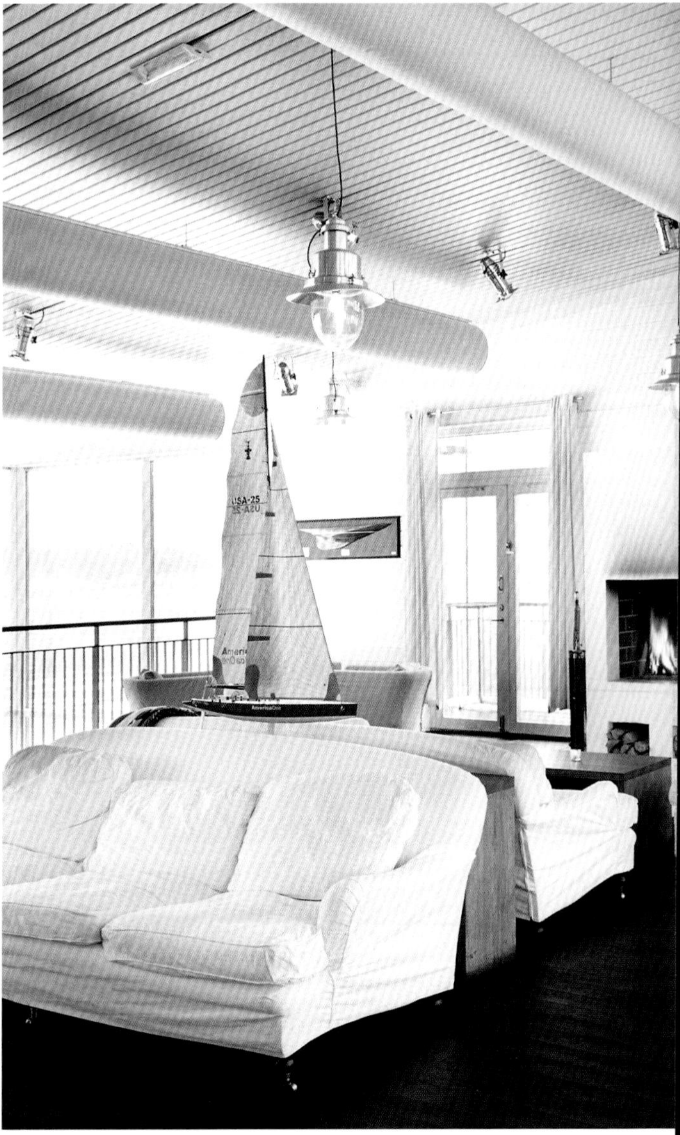
USA-25

Gåshaga
Situated 15 minutes by car or 30 by train
or boat from the city centre, the hotel
has only 13 rooms, each with a balcony
and sea view. The décor was inspired by
a summer house in Newport, USA, and
the open fires and thick blankets may
well make you feel like you're in a Ralph
Lauren advert. Not such a bad thing.
Värdshusvägen 14-16, Lidingö,
T 601 3400, www.gashaga.nu

Berns Hotel

Traditionally recognised as the hippest and most centrally located hotel in the city, it was the attached chichi, celebrity-filled nightclub that made this place's reputation. These days, the Berns may have matured, but there's no sign of its popularity or looks fading – the club has reopened after a major refit, there's a live-music schedule on the bar terrace in summer and a top-notch Asian kitchen.

We recommend you book an X-Large Room (above), which have huge terraces for hosting private soirées, while the Clock Suite, with views from the galleried bedroom overlooking most of Stockholm, is an ideal place to wake up.
Näckströmsgatan 8, T 5663 2200, www.berns.se

Hotel Esplanade

If you like your hotels to have character, then look no further. The Esplanade's lobby is full of pictures of how it looked when it opened in 1910 as short-term, serviced apartments, done up in the Jugendstil, and not much has changed since. Gentle renovations over the years have given each room an en-suite bathroom, much of the furniture has been upholstered and a small sauna was added, but the incredible art nouveau parquet flooring, wood panelling and fireplaces remain perfectly intact, as in room 14 (above). In short, what the place lacks in hi-tech gadgets and bathtub size, it more than makes up for in old-fashioned Scandinavian charm.
Strandvägen 7a, T 663 0740,
www.hotelesplanade.se

Story Hotel

Opened in March 2009, this bohemian 82-room boutique hotel is located in Stureplan, just a few steps from the renowned shopping district of Östermalm. The hotel, which is a mixture of downtown New York meets Parisian salon, has been a welcome addition to the capital. The interior is a blend of industrial chic and classic opulence whose features include exposed pipes, concrete floors and pillars, velvet furnishings and Wonderwall photographs and prints, also available for purchase from the hotel's gift shop. The hotel includes a bar and lounge (above) with a resident weekend DJ and a restaurant, which serves small plates designed to be shared. Story offers 12 room types, ranging from Super Squeeze to the spacious Lily Dam Suite (opposite), so be sure to select your preference.
Riddargatan 6, T 5450 3940,
www.storyhotels.com

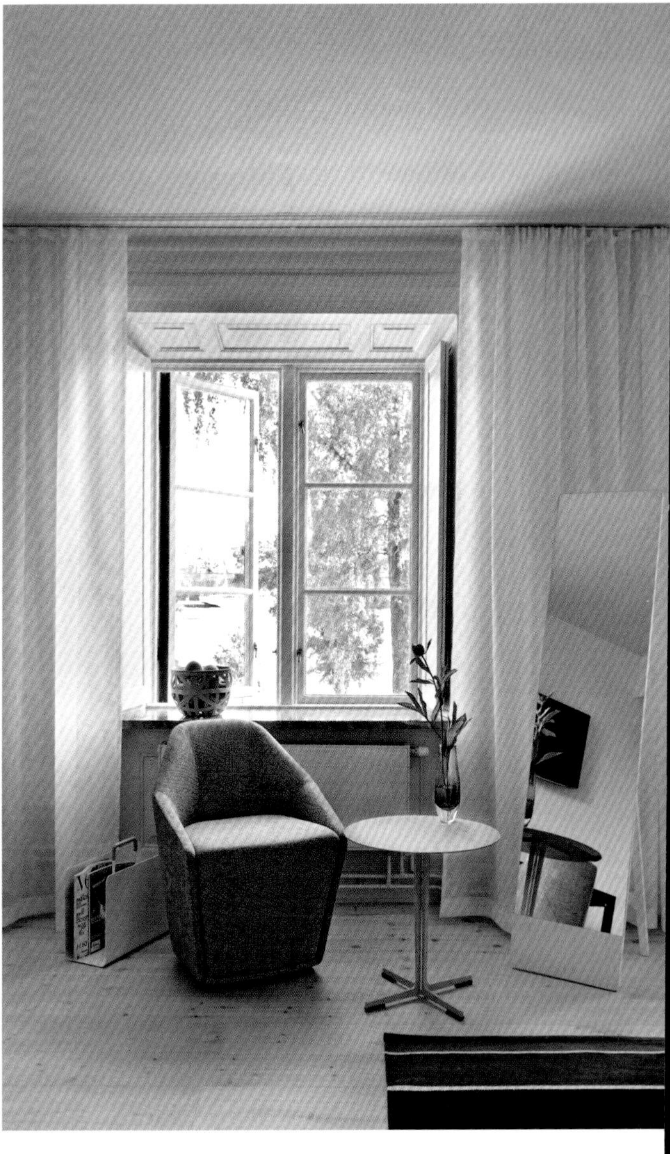

Skeppsholmen
Situated on one of the most picturesque
of the Stockholm isles, this 81-room
hotel is the perfect destination should
you be looking for a little peace. Housed
in two historical barracks built in 1699, it
was designed by Claesson Koivisto Rune
in collaboration with Erséus Architects.
We recommend room 254 (pictured).
Gröna Gången 1, T 440 5241,
www.hotelskeppsholmen.se

Grand Hôtel

Rich, opulent and boasting a guest list that includes most of the royalty, heads of state and superstars ever to visit the city, this is one hotel that lives up to its name. Despite the reputation, the Grand refuses to rest on its laurels. In 2006, 76 new rooms opened in Burmanska Palace next door, including a new penthouse suite. An exclusive restaurant and renovated caviar bar set the scene in the lobby, while views over the harbour from the south side are breathtaking. Should you find the heavy Gustavian style of the Bernadotte Suite too much, there are six Superior Suites, one of which, Room 150, is done up with Svenskt Tenn fabrics and furniture, while Deluxe Room 5503 (above) is charmingly feminine.
Södra Blasieholmshamnen 8, T 679 3500, www.grandhotel.se

Clarion Hotel Sign

Designed by local architect Gert Wingårdh and opened in 2008, the glazed black Clarion stands in the middle of the recently developed Norra Bantorget district. One of the city's largest hotels with 558 rooms, it's not for those seeking a cosy, boutique atmosphere. However, you will find Nordic furnishings and immaculate design. All of the rooms on the fourth floor have sofas or chairs by Norway Says, while the fifth floor is dedicated to Alvar Aalto. Rooms on floors six to 10, such as Superior Room 1005 (above), feature classics such as Arne Jacobsen's 'Egg' chair or Erik Jørgensen's 'EJ250' sofa. Fans of Hans J Wegner's 'Ox' chair should book Suite 601. The real treat, however, is on the roof: the heated outdoor pool means you can even swim in winter.
Östra Järnvägsgatan 35, T 676 9800, www.clarionsign.com

Lydmar
Featuring views of Blasieholmen, Old
Town and the Royal Palace, you would
be hard-pressed to find a better location.
The rooms are spacious, such as the
X-Large (above), and the restaurant is
one the most popular in the city, which
might explain why it has become a
haunt for the *beau monde*.
Södra Blasieholmshamnen 2, T 223 160,
www.lydmar.com

24 HOURS

SEE THE BEST OF THE CITY IN JUST ONE DAY

Stockholm is a city of climatic contrast, with temperatures falling to -10 °C in the winter months and climbing to a bright 25 °C with close to 24 hours of daylight in the summer, rendering a complete transformation. Equally notable is the city's ability to go from tranquil, bucolic landscape to bustling shopping district in only a few minutes. These extremes unite rather than divide the city, as Stockholmers embrace their separate seasons with gusto.

Regardless of the season, a visit to the pretty, peaceful island of Djurgården can't fail to put you in a good mood. A half-hour stroll through the woods is a glorious start to any day. Swedish breakfast is also a divine experience to be savoured. While pickled fish, strong cheese and crackerbread continue to divide foreigners' tastes, the speciality bread and pastries always go down well. Try Albert & Jacks (see p034), a local favourite just a stone's throw away from the cutting-edge shops of nearby Södermalm. Head to Östermalm for some of Europe's finest design showrooms and boutiques, although you may want to stop in Norrmalm for lunch. The area is packed with choice, such as KonstnärsBaren (see p058), located in the heart of the city's shopping boulevard. Finally, after drinks at Lilla Baren (see p038), head back to Gamla Stan for dinner – the snug, old-world atmosphere at Kaffekoppen (Stortorget 20, T 203 170) means it shouldn't be missed.
For full addresses, see Resources.

08.30 Djurgården

Djurgården is one of the 14 islands that make up Stockholm city, but that's as far as its association with the word 'city' goes. A lushly wooded park, lined with shaded walkways, grassy knolls and waterside pathways, a light jog or stroll under the emerald green canopy of Djurgården's trees (and should the weather allow, a quick dip in the water) is the ideal way to start the day. Located amid this parkland are the zoo, circus, museums and various restaurants; one of the cosiest is Djurgårdsbrunn (T 624 2200) which sits just next to the canal.

10.00 Albert & Jacks

In a city without a deli culture, Albert & Jacks is quite a find. Stockholmers flock here for both breakfast and lunch. Serving fresh ingredients, daily baked breads and exclusively blended teas and coffee, it is little wonder that the shop has gained such popularity. Situated in an old dock house, dating back to 1640, this deli-cum-bakery is located in the Old Town, nestled among the charming cobbled alleyways of Gamla Stan. Overlooking the Stockholm bay, the venue is well worth the trip for a macchiato and brioche, or a take-away sandwich to be enjoyed by the waterfront. After brunch, take a look around the numerous galleries that line the street of Österlanggatan. A second branch can be found in the exclusive neighbourhood of Östermalm island, but we prefer the original location.
Skeppsbron 24, T 411 5045,
www.albertjacks.com

13.00 Konsthantverkarna

After 55 years at its previous premises, Konsthantverkarna's boutique moved to its trendy new location by Slussen in late 2005, taking on a savvy new persona in the process. A kind of union for professional Swedish craftsmen working in glass, sculpture, ceramics, textiles, jewellery, silver, wood and leather, the 70 artists that make up Konsthantverkarna have cast off old-fashioned handiwork in favour of slick, high-quality design. With the shop filled to the brim with table-top pieces and utensils, as well as exclusive objets d'art, jewellery and ceramics, this is as much a gallery to go to for inspiration as it is a shop. Refuel with lunch at Gondolen (T 641 7090), just a short stroll away.
Södermalmstorg 4, T 611 0370, www.konsthantverkarna.se

16.00 Gamla Lampor

Stockholm's vast landscape is strewn with some of the finest retail wonders in Europe. Start at the distinctive Svenskt Tenn (see p083) and continue walking to Gamla Lampor (above) on Nybrogatan, where fine vintage lamps looking for good homes blanket the walls and ceilings. Carry on to Östermalmstorg to Modernity (see p082), a treasure trove of Scandinavian vintage furniture and glassware. Asplund

(see p076), a couple of blocks further up Sibyllegatan, houses the best in Swedish contemporary design and will tempt even the most hardened maximalist to embrace Scandinavian minimalism.
Almlöfsgatan 3, T 611 9035

18.00 Fotografiska

Stockholm's first and only photography museum is located in a fantastic art nouveau building by Ferdinand Boberg. The old customs house, which dates from 1906, was converted into a vast museum in 2010 by two Swedish architecture practices, AIX Architects and Guise. It shows four major photo exhibitions per year – since opening in 2010 it has headlined international stars such as Annie Leibovitz, Albert Watson (above) and Robert Mapplethorpe – but this is also the place to see cutting-edge work by local photographers. While here, don't forget to pay a visit to the well-stocked bookshop and marvel at the view across Stockholm's archipelago from the bar and restaurant's panoramic windows. *Stadsgårdshamnen 22, T 5090 0500, www.fotografiska.eu*

19.30 Lilla Baren

This isn't the place for a quiet, intimate evening *à deux*. Jostling for space in this small but perfectly formed bar are Stockholm's hottest party people. A mix of pure posh and creative media types, this is the drinking den to spot famous actors and musicians. Think T-shirts, blazers and slicked-back hair. Restaurang Riche (T 5450 3560) next door, housed in an 1890s mansion and designed by Jonas Bohlin, is also worth a visit and attracts the same chichi crowd.
Birger Jarlsgatan 4, T 5450 3560, www.riche.se

URBAN LIFE
CAFÉS, RESTAURANTS, BARS AND NIGHTCLUBS

There is a theory that Swedes hanker after great interior design because they have dinner parties rather than go out. This is easily disproved by a night on the tiles in the capital. Aside from perhaps Sundays – when many of the restaurants are closed – Stockholm's eateries are always packed (booking is essential on Fridays and Saturdays). True, it's not cheap and the infamous Scandinavian alcohol prices are scary, but in return the quality is outstanding. Food is fresh, menus are very exciting and most of the high-end restaurants have wine cellars to rival the finest establishments in New York and Paris. Competition between nightspots is fierce, with hot new venues opening up all the time.

What hasn't changed is the Swedish love affair with coffee, cake and a good gossip. The notion of *fika* ('to have coffee'), along with Stockholm's prowess at keeping the corporate coffeehouse chains off the high streets, has created a vibrant café culture. For nightlife, however, Stockholm is fairly conservative during the week. Bars are open daily, usually until midnight or 1am, but tend to stay quiet until Thursday, Friday and Saturday when the party goes on well into the early hours and queuing is routine. It's also worth being aware of the differing dress codes across the city – from the smart suited-and-booted style in the bars in Östermalm to the vintage, dress-down look in Södermalm.

For full addresses, see Resources.

Restaurang AG

It doesn't take long to figure out what Restaurang AG is all about. At the entrance, large cuts of meat hang in a huge glass refrigerator, accompanied by thousands of bottles of wine. Head chef Johan Jureskog and his business partner Klas Ljungquist, who also co-owns restaurant Rolfs Kök (T 101 696), took over AG in 2011 and commissioned local designer Jonas Bohlin to design the interiors. Some of the best meat in the world is served here, with a menu featuring entrecôte of Black Angus beef from the US, Iberico Bellota from Spain and lamb from Välnäs served with a dill sauce, a Swedish classic. The signature dish is the burger 'Jureskog's Way', which is served with extra cheese and bacon, and is considered by many to be the city's finest. *Kronobergsgatan 37, T 4106 8100, www.restaurangag.se*

Esperanto

Opened in November 2005, Esperanto's simple, no-frills concept of good food, good venue and good service has caught on with locals. Determined not to be placed in any one culinary category, the owners came up with the name of the establishment on the basis that food is an international language. The menu is therefore based on which ingredients go best together and, to keep it simple, there are only two choices you have to make: seven courses or eight. Dishes are small but perfectly formed, with past delights including the delectable pigeon 'ras-el-hanout' and melt-in-your-mouth whipped brie with truffle bread, while the carefully chosen wine menu offers a different grape to go with each.
Kungstensgatan 2, T 696 2323, www.esperantorestaurant.se

Operakällaren

The direct translation may be 'opera cellar' but this is no dingy basement. Set on the ground floor with views over the water to the palace, the dining room is nothing short of a fairy tale. In late 2005 the place was given a facelift by darlings of the local architecture world Claesson Koivisto Rune who, while praised for their clever use of huge golden mirrors to make full use of the exquisite ceiling and stunning chandeliers, have come in for criticism with their upholstered chairs and lights. Love it or loathe it, the refurb has brought the place back onto the A-list, and while you're bound to find the odd tourist within its carved oak walls, this is no reason to miss out on the place that (still) makes the locals most proud.
Operahuset, Karl XII:s Torg, T 676 5800, www.operakallaren.se

Nytorget Urban Deli

Breakfast, lunch, dinner, takeaway: it's all here at Nytorget Urban Deli. This laidback spot is a big favourite among Södermalm's trendy 30-somethings, with raw concrete walls and metallic chairs giving this former post office an industrial feel. The menu mixes French, American and Swedish cuisine, and features dishes such as steak tartare, Toast Skagen, a Swedish classic consisting of shrimp, mayonnaise and dill served on fried toast and home-made sausage. As well as a bar, the venue also includes a deli in case you want to get some of the charcuterie or freshly baked bread to take away.
Nytorget 4, T 5990 9180,
www.urbandeli.org

Råkultur

Helmed by Swedish star chef Sayan
Isaksson – who also runs Esperanto (see
p044), conveniently located a few floors
above in this listed building – Råkultur
is said to serve the best sushi in the city.
Isaksson's unique way of interpreting
flavours and seasoning with imagination
has placed him well ahead of the game.
Unfortunately, Råkultur, meaning Raw
Culture, is only open for lunch and queues
start forming around the block as early as
11am, so get in early or call ahead for a
takeaway. Try the *moriawase*; beautifully
presented sashimi in a box.
*Kungstensgatan 2, T 696 2325,
www.rakultur.se*

PA&Co

Perched on a quiet corner of Östermalm, this die-hard diner has been serving *husmanskost* (hearty Swedish fare) to perfection for 20 years. Every night, from 7pm, the restaurant is a busy spot to see and be seen, and on any day of the week you will notice a large crowd of hopefuls waiting for a table by the bar. Inside the intimate bistro the atmosphere is cosy and continental, surprisingly well aged.

Scrawled on a large chalkboard is a hardly legible menu, but those in the know will skip a look at the board and simply order the usual. Try Beef Rydberg.
Riddargatan 8, T 611 0845,
www.paco.se

Frantzén/Lindeberg

In January 2008, chefs Bjorn Frantzén & Daniel Lindeberg opened what may quite possibly be the best restaurant in town. Don't let its appearance fool you; although it may look like a modest 'at home' setting that seats only 19, the culinary experience is something different altogether. The menu is wildly inventive, incorporating ingredients such as bee pollen, lavender and truffle tea. Without wishing to give too much of the show away, smoke effects are big and some of the dishes are served scentless with their aroma brought separately in a paper bag on the side. What can we say – one simply has to experience it.
Lilla Nygatan 21, T 208 580,
www.frantzen-lindeberg.com

Baren at Lydmar
This bar is packed with fashion, music and advertising types on most nights. It is a place considered so cool by locals that it doesn't even need to bother with putting its name on the door. Located in the middle of the shopping and financial district, it offers great cocktails and live jazz. Check the website for concert dates.
Södra Blasieholmshamnen 2,
T 223 160, www.lydmar.com

BAR

Short for Blasieholmens Akvarium o Restaurang, BAR is the sister restaurant of Michelin-starred restaurant Lux (T 619 0190), and is certainly the more approachable of the two. Opened in 2009, the roomy dining hall was designed by local architecture firm Koncept, who were also behind Story Hotel (see p024). Featuring generous windows, white-tiled walls and oak tables, BAR has an informal food-hall feel, with daily specials written directly onto blackboards and mirrors. Fresh seafood is your best bet, although there are also meat and vegetarian options on the menu. Go for the popular crispy cod with French fries, or for a more unusual choice, try the nettle soup with smoked char and a poached egg.
Blasieholmsgatan 4a, T 611 5335, www.restaurangbar.se

Pontus

Pontus Frithiof, chef and restaurateur, is true culinary royalty in Stockholm. He opened his first eaterie at the age of 27 after training in Paris from the age of 15 under award-winning Swedish chefs Leif Mannerstrom and Erik Lallerstedt. The restaurant, with its perfectly cooked seasonal food, is just part of the Pontus experience. The venue also includes an oyster bar, claiming to sell the best oysters and champagne in town, and a cocktail bar serving Asian delicacies. Considering all there is on offer, it's little wonder Pontus has become a favourite with locals and visitors alike.
Brunnsgatan 1, T 5452 7300,
www.pontusfrithiof.com

Den Gyldene Freden

Dating back to 1722, Den Gyldene Freden, meaning 'Golden Peace', was named in honour of the peace treaty signed the previous year at Nystad, which ended the Great Northern War. Today it is owned by the Swedish Academy that selects the Nobel Prize for Literature and, rumour has it, many a prize has been decided here. A favourite of artists, writers and poets for obvious reasons, the menu is also a draw with its mix of traditional Swedish cooking and more innovative inventions, such as beef carpaccio and goat's cheese on toast with citrus salsa, and rose-hip soup with vanilla ice-cream. *Österlånggatan 51, T 249 760, www.gyldenefreden.se*

KonstnärsBaren

KonstnärsBaren (meaning 'Artist Bar') is as popular today as it was in the 1930s when it first opened. This is a classic Swedish bistro and the preferred haunt of artists, actors and hacks, beautifully preserved in its original shape and form; even the tables and chairs date back to 1932. The restaurant is housed in a building called Konstnärshuset ('Artist House') and includes five floors of gallery space that house exhibitions throughout the year, while the restaurant itself is adorned with art and murals painted over the decades. We recommend the four types of pickled herring – a house speciality – for a starter and the veal burger to follow. Be sure to book ahead; lunchtimes, in particular, get very busy.
Smålandsgatan 7, T 679 6032,
www.konstnarsbaren.se

Teatergrillen

This no-windows restaurant, complete with low lighting, red velvet booths and stone walls, comes as close to power dining, mafia-style, as it gets in Sweden. Taking full advantage of its proximity to Dramaten (the magnificent theatre founded by King Gustav III in 1788 for Swedish dramas to be performed in their original language), the interior takes on a luxurious *Moulin Rouge* feel, with a collection of masks and costumes and a frieze depicting a stunning view over the rooftops of Paris. Ask for the corner booth (table 53), order the salt-baked entrecôte with béarnaise, warm horseradish and pommes Pont Neuf, then head next door to aristocratic members' club Noppe's Bar (T 8678 1030) to clinch the deal.
Nybrogatan 3, T 5450 3565,
www.teatergrillen.se

Matbaren
Literally 'The Food Bar', Matbaren
is one half of Restaurant Mathias
Dahlgren at the Grand Hôtel (see p028).
With a Michelin star to its name – the
other half of the eatery, Matsalen,
('The Dining Room') has two – it's a
good place to enjoy innovative and
exquisite dishes in a relaxed setting.
Södra Blasieholmshamnen 6,
T 679 3584, www.mathiasdahlgren.com

INSIDER'S GUIDE

CAMILLA MODIN DJANAIEFF, PR DIRECTOR

As director of communication and lifestyle agency Modinåkerlind, our Stockholm girl-about-town, Camilla Modin Djanaieff, has her fingers in just about every pie going. Her extensive list of clients includes Berns, Malmsten and Byredo perfumes among others. When asked what she loves most about Stockholm, she says: 'The luxury of living in a city and still being able to be so close to nature and the water.' A resident of the chic Östermalm district, a typical Saturday starts with a coffee at Riddarbageriet (Riddargatan 15, T 660 3375), followed either by a jog around Djurgården (see p033) or a yoga session at Yoga Yama (Jungfrugatan 8, T 660 8860). Then she'll have lunch with friends at either Restaurang Riche (see p039) or at Lisa Elmqvist (T 5534 0400) inside Östermalms Saluhall (see p084). 'It's also the best place to pick fresh oysters and seafood for dinner.' If she and her husband decide to go out for a meal, they usually head to PA&Co (see p048) after having had a pre-prandial cocktail at Cadierbaren in the Grand Hôtel (p028).

Djanaieff also recommends a visit to Moderna Museet (see p010) as well as the smaller galleries along Hudiksvallsgatan and Gallery Charlotte Lund (Kungstensgatan 23, T 663 0979). Her favourite shopping venues are Nathalie Schuterman (Birger Jarlsgatan 5, T 611 6201), Rodebjer (see p077) and Saker & Ting (Sturegatan 28, T 667 3763) for quirky vintage pieces.

For full addresses, see Resources.

ARCHITOUR

A GUIDE TO STOCKHOLM'S ICONIC BUILDINGS

When the Social Democratic Party implemented its progressive reforms in 1932, public housing projects were highlighted as Swedish architecture's main task. Stockholm's landscape waved goodbye to the elaborate neoclassical buildings made popular at the turn of the century by architects such as Ivar Tengbom and Erik Gunnar Asplund in favour of stern, modern projects that embraced a functionalist aesthetic. A strict government agenda meant that gaining planning permission for individuals became almost impossible, and with ambitious projects such as the Million Homes Programme between 1965 and 1975, few architects were given much scope to experiment and shine, with the exception of Celsing's super-modern structure Kulturhuset (see p015) of 1974.

Aside from a brief building boom in the late 1980s that saw private developers take a leading role, it wasn't until the mid-1990s that new and intriguing modern structures started to crop up. The change may be slow, but it is definitely steady. The rapid growth of the IT industry generated demand for new office space and with several young and interesting architecture practices set up in the city (for example White Architects and Sandellsandberg), as well as a keen interest in getting foreign architects (such as Foster + Partners) involved in shaping the landscape, Stockholm is starting to gain the forward-thinking landmarks it deserves. *For full addresses, see Resources.*

Gåshaga Brygga

This exclusive residential complex on the island of Lidingö set new standards for affluent living standards when it opened in 2001. Designed by architect Thomas Sandell in conjunction with NCC, it is made up of 40 elegant two- and three-storey houses, some with cantilevered sections over the water. Plain concrete exteriors reveal stunning, individually designed minimal interiors complete with large windows, spacious terraces, open layouts and private mooring points. Unusually, the development evolved from landowners and not the municipality. With wonderful views and a relaxing atmosphere, these units are among the most extravagant of the city's recent housing projects.
Gåshaga Brygga 13, www.boende.ncc.se

Lending Hall, Stadsbiblioteket

Erik Gunnar Asplund's last building to embrace Nordic classicism also borrows forms and ornament from ancient Egypt. A processional path from the entrance leads up the stairs into the magnificent broad cylindrical sphere. Stockholm's public library is perhaps the capital's most internationally acclaimed building. *Sveavägen 73, T 5083 1100, www.ssb.stockholm.se*

Millesgården
Former home and studio of Swedish sculptor Carl Milles, Millesgården was designed by Carl M Bengtsson. Although the original house was built in 1908, it was followed by almost half a century of expansion. Today the site is a museum featuring Milles's major works, as well as his collection of Greek and Roman art.
Herserudsvägen 32, Lidingö,
T 446 7590, www.millesgarden.se

Stadshuset

Perhaps Stockholm's most iconic building, City Hall was commissioned in 1907. The city held an architectural contest that in the end came down to Swedish architects Ragner Östberg and Carl Westman. Östberg won the commission, but continually altered his initial design. Indeed, the Blue Hall (above) never received the blue tiles which formed part of the original plan, although it did keep the name. Today, the hall is by far the most exclusive ballroom in Stockholm, host to State visits and the annual Nobel Prize award ceremony. Do have a look at the organ in the hall comprising 10,270 pipes, the largest in Scandinavia.
Hantverkargatan 1, T 5082 9000, www.stockholm.se/cityhall

SHOPPING

THE BEST RETAIL THERAPY AND WHAT TO BUY

Scandinavian design has undergone something of a renaissance in the last couple of years, with Sweden as the major player. Be it established contemporary names such as CKR, Thomas Sandell and Jonas Bohlin, classics from favourites like Josef Frank, Bruno Mathsson and Erik Gunnar Asplund or fresh, innovative products by the likes of David & Martin, Monica Förster and Anna Kraitz, Stockholm has them all. And, unlike many other cities, most of the top design showrooms are within walking distance of each other.

Swedish fashion may be less renowned, but when it comes to original, wearable, high-quality clothes, the Stockholm high street is hard to beat. While brands like Acne (see p078) and Filippa K (Grev Turegatan 18, T 5458 8888) are making their mark internationally, they are cheaper when buying in Swedish kronor. Less well-known abroad but equally hot locally is preppy Whyred (Mäster Samuelsgatan 3, T 660 0170), and the Fifth Avenue Shoe Repair (see p086) outlet in Norrmalm is outstanding. Nitty Gritty (Krukmakargatan 24-26, T 658 2440) and Kocksgatan 17 (Kocksgatan 17, T 8408 15014) stock global favourites such as Polo Ralph Lauren and APC, but the collections are superbly edited and displayed in fanciful and fresh interiors. Don't forget a shopping day in Stockholm would be incomplete without visiting a design shop such as Modernity (see p082).

For full addresses, see Resources.

Snickarbacken 7

Located in the stable of a former Catholic
girls' school, this concept store is worth
a visit for the interior alone. A gallery and
a café share the space, which features
original wooden doors and vaulted ceilings
from the late 1700s, along with five design
and fashion retailers. These include
independent brands from Sweden and
elsewhere – Swedish furniture producer
David Design sells pieces made by Nordic
names such as Matti Klenell and Jonas
Wagell while Van Deurs Et Al offers
sophisticated evening wear. Be sure to
try the cappuccino at the cafe, Kaffeverket,
which specialises in coffee from da Matteo,
the Gothenburg-based micro-roastery.
*Snickarbacken 7, T 070 738 8394,
www.snickarbacken7.se*

Byredo

Byredo is a rare independent success in a perfume industry dominated by the international fashion houses. The brand was founded in 2006 by Ben Gorham, and business quickly took off when its products were stocked by Colette in Paris. Byredo's success is easy to understand: its selection of pure scents, some with only five core ingredients, stand out from the mass of industrially produced fragrances. The flagship store in Stockholm (opposite) features a beautiful interior created by local designers Christian Halleröd and Johannes Svartholm, and offers the full range of intriguingly named perfumes, such as the intensely fruity 'Pulp' (above, SEK1,400), alongside scented candles and body products.
Mäster Samuelsgatan 6, T 5250 2615, www.byredo.com

Asplund

Brothers Michael and Thomas Asplund have been supplying stylish Stockholmers with clean, elegant furniture for over two decades. Stocking both contemporary classics as well as their own commissions from Sweden's top creatives, Asplund has launched several careers, including those of Ola Wihlborg and Stina Sandwall, and has also produced new ranges by old favourites such as Claesson Koivisto Rune and Thomas Sandell. While it skirts around the experimental and conceptual aspects of modern Swedish design, it remains a testament to high-quality, functional and chic Scandinavian style.
Sibyllegatan 31, T 662 5284, www.asplund.org

Rodebjer

The 67-sq-m Rodebjer flagship store opened in August 2007 and is located on the busy side street of the main shopping artery of Biblioteksgatan. Although the brand is now available in most big cities around the world, it is still worth a visit if only to see Carin Rodebjer's strong shapes and slightly dark romantic garments at home in this little gem of a store. The design of the shop was a collective effort between A1 architects and illustrator and set designer Liselotte Watkins. We couldn't help but pick up the simple, yet flirtatious 'Higgins' T-shirt (above, SEK499). After shopping, make your way to Sosta Espresso Bar (T 611 7107) across the street, which is a local favourite of the in crowd.
Jakobsbergsgatan 6, T 4104 6095, www.rodebjer.com

Acne

Started in 1997 by Stockholm-based design firm Ambition to Create Novel Expressions, Acne Jeans' signature red stitching and minimalist Scandinavian style received global attention almost overnight. Although the brand is now represented worldwide, we recommend a visit to its flagship store (pictured). *Norrmalmstorg 2, T 611 6411, www.acnestudios.com*

Rehns Antikhandel

A fantastic eclectic mix of coveted design collectables, antiques, art and lighting, this is the Alfie's market of Stockholm. The ample crystal chandeliers dangle over Gustavian dining tables, painted in lime green and laden with Memphis and Fornasetti porcelain, while old backdrops with scenes from the opera transform into art. The drama and eccentricity are heightened by the fact that the gallery is housed in an old turn-of-the-century theatre and clever styling stops it from crossing the line into kitsch.
Sibyllegatan 26, T 663 3451

Modernity

Originally in Gamla Stan, Modernity moved to this spacious central location in April 2003. Since then the showroom has gone from strength to strength, largely due to the good taste and passion of its owner – not a Swede but a Scotsman, Andrew Duncanson. Famed the world over for its fine vintage collection, particularly by the grand masters of the Scandinavian style, such as Wegner, Mathsson, Aalto, Juhl, Jacobsen, Wirkkala and Sarpaneva, it is the occasional limited editions by various established Swedish designers like Mats Theselius and Jonas Bohlin that are really worth fighting over. Mixed in with these renowned names you will also find emerging contemporary designers, such as Caroline Schlyter. *Sibyllegatan 6, T 208 025, www.modernity.se*

Svenskt Tenn

Despite the presence of Svenskt Tenn in London and New York, a trip to its flagship Strandvägen boutique is a totally different experience, especially since its extensive 2011 refurbishment. Set up in 1924 by Josef Frank and Estrid Ericson, Svenskt Tenn is an idea, a lifestyle – perhaps even a distinct culture in its own right. Keen to preserve its legacy, the directors are reissuing new pieces and textiles from Frank's archives every year, as well as keeping the spirit of Estrid alive in the imaginative window displays and décor. That said, contemporary talents are very involved in the new collections, and the store buys heavily from Scandinavian designers, such as this teapot 'Myrten' (above, SEK1,700) by Signe Persson Melin. *Strandvägen 5, T 670 1600, www.svenskttenn.se*

Östermalms Saluhall
Since opening in 1888, generations of gourmands have visited Östermalms Saluhall on the corner of Östermalmstorg to pick up everything from simple foods, such as bread and cheese, to reindeer meat and bleak roe. One can easily spend a couple of hours beneath the glass ceilings of this market just walking around, sampling all the fare and watching the locals fight their way to the counters for the best cuts. Visit Lisa Elmqvist (T 5534 0400), the finest stall for fish and seafood, where you can also dine at the counter on the catch of the day. For meat, game and grouse, B Andersson Fågel & Vilt (T 662 5557) is unsurpassed, while Robert's Coffee (T 662 5106) grinds fresh beans for every cup of coffee it serves, and Nybroe Smørrebrød (T 662 2320) has some of the best open sandwiches in Stockholm – try the daily trio.
Östermalmstorg, www.ostermalmshallen.se

Fifth Avenue Shoe Repair

Named after a historic shoemaker's shop in London, Fifth Avenue Shoe Repair was founded in 2004 by Astrid Olsson and Lee Cotter and focused on delicate women's knits and jerseys. Today, it is internationally renowned as a leading designer in men's and women's tailoring. The brand's experimental cuts and dramatic draping have helped establish its iconic image. In 2009 the label celebrated the opening of a second outlet at Mäster Samuelsgatan 2 (above). The new concept store was designed by architectural firm Guise, which used the brand's style and design as the inspiration for the interior setting. *Mäster Samuelsgatan 2, T 611 1640, www.shoerepair.se*

Designgalleriet

Housed in a tiny space in the Vasastaden neighbourhood, this gallery devotes itself to promoting interior, graphic, fashion and product design. We spotted a few interesting pieces including this 'Bush for God' chair (above, SEK15,000). Inspired by Moss in New York and Vessel in London, Designgalleriet was designed by the Stockholm-based industrial design studio Form Us With Love, who divided the space using black foam and sound-absorbing tubes, which allow for easy conversion of the space. Through its ever-changing schedule of exhibitions, ranging from university graduate shows to established international designers, the gallery keeps reinventing itself and manages to keep content fresh.
*Odengatan 21, T 230 021,
www.designgalleriet.com*

SPORTS AND SPAS
WORK OUT, CHILL OUT OR JUST WATCH

Considering its small population, Sweden's success in global sports is remarkable. Activities such as tennis, skiing, athletics, ice hockey and golf regularly seem to produce world champions. In part, this is due to the nation's enthusiasm for keeping fit. Stockholm offers fantastic indoor facilities – such as the 16 indoor courts at the Royal Lawn Tennis Club (see p090), Centralbadet (Drottninggatan 88, T 5452 1300), which puts most other city pools to shame, and the fabulously equipped Sturebadet gym (see p094). And with a winter landscape that offers long-distance ice-skating, cross-country skiing, ice hockey and ice fishing just a 10-minute drive from the centre, locals would never let the cold get in the way of staying active. As the old Scandic saying goes: 'There's no such thing as bad weather, just bad clothes.'

Come summer, however, and the Swedes' dedication to staying outside and enjoying the few weeks of glorious sunshine means a great plethora of al fresco activities. Every Stockholmer has their personal favourite bathing spot – be it the large Fågelöudde beach on Lidingö complete with water slides, diving boards and saunas or a hidden little rock on Kastellholmen. The city's proximity to the wet stuff also means that watersports are very popular, with fishing and sailing high on the summer agenda. On land, bicycles are the preferred mode of transportation.

For full addresses, see Resources.

Yasuragi Spa

Admittedly the coaches in the car park might be a turn-off, but this Japanese-inspired spa is popular for good reason. With changing rooms you can get lost in, a large indoor pool, inside and outdoor jacuzzis, several saunas and steam rooms, treatments galore and classes in everything from meditation to sushi-making, there's something for everyone. Yasuragi does sacrifice cosy for all-encompassing, but if you're looking for snug, the unisex steam room should be able to provide just that and more.
Hamndalsvägen 6, Saltsjö-Boo, T 747 6100, www.yasuragi.se

Royal Lawn Tennis Club
Although founded in 1896 by the Crown
Prince Gustaf V (an enthusiastic tennis
player), the actual hall was not built
until 1943. Today the club includes 16
indoor hard courts, five outdoor clay
courts and eight squash courts. It is
home to the If Stockholm Open and has
played host to the odd concert, including
the Beatles and the Rolling Stones.
Lidingövägen 75, T 459 1500

Balance

A gym that lacks nothing and is the first of its kind in Stockholm, Balance is an upmarket sweatshop decked out with rows of shiny machines & VIP training rooms. Opened in 2006, this branch is one of two in the city. It was designed by Ahlsén Architects who are also responsible for the extension of the Grand Hôtel (see p028) and collaborated with Ilse Crawford on Restaurant Mathias Dahlgren (see p060).

Balance is owned by Daniel Westling, a personal training guru now turned fitness and health entrepreneur, who in 2010 married Crown Princess Victoria. *Lästmakargatan 10, T 407 4400, www.balancetraining.se*

Ericsson Globe

Measuring 110m in diameter and 85m high, the Ericsson Globe is still the largest spherical building in the world since its opening in 1989. Sweden's main sporting venue holds 16,500 fans and has placed the country on the map as a destination for rock concerts and sporting events. Known by locals as the giant golf ball, the arena is sometimes used for ice hockey and innebandy (or floorball as the sport is known internationally). Both are great spectator sports and worth seeing live to get a sense of Stockholm's sports culture. *Globentorget 2, T 771 310 000, www.globearenas.se*

Sturebadet
This luxurious gym, swimming pool and spa complex was founded in 1885 by Carl Curman. A members-only club, guest day passes are available, though numbers are strictly limited. This is the place to enjoy an Arctic spa treatment, massage or facial; it is certainly a favourite retreat with celebrity types.
Sturegallerian 36, T 5450 1500
www.sturebadet.se

ESCAPES

WHERE TO GO IF YOU WANT TO LEAVE TOWN

For all of Stockholm's attempts to come across as metropolitan, you just know she's a country girl at heart. The city's in such easy reach of so many places of pristine natural beauty that it seems criminal not to take advantage. Most spectacular is the vast and unique fan-shaped archipelago that stretches out more than 100km from Saltsjön into a magical island world. Known as the 'urban wilderness', the area consists of more than 24,000 islands of which only about a thousand are inhabited. A boater's paradise, with speedboats and yachts for rent, this span of water is also easily accessed by the several ferries that depart regularly from central Stockholm. Whether you're after a short day trip or a couple of nights' break, the archipelago offers a wide selection of some of the best hotels and restaurants in Scandinavia.

While some larger establishments are open all year round, most, like Oaxen Krog (Mörkö, T 5515 3105), tend to be limited to the summer. Extended daylight hours and balmy weather mean early May to the end of August are the peak times to head out to the archipelago, but winter can offer just as spectacular scenery, with ice-skating and warming up in front of cosy fires being high on the agenda. Alternatively, if you're after something more extreme, the north of Sweden has some of the most challenging and well-maintained ski slopes in Europe.

For full addresses, see Resources.

Sandhamn

You may recognise the name from the Stieg Larsson trilogy and, yes, it actually exists. Accessible only by boat or ferry, this island comes alive from April until September when the yachting season gets under way on the Swedish east coast, and is a must for sailing enthusiasts. Sandhamn is also the start and finishing line for the Eurocard Round Gotland Race, one of the world's largest offshore races.

But you don't have to be a sailor to enjoy the island; there are also some spectacular, long, sandy beaches. Trouville, a 15-minute walk from the harbour, is one of the best. Stay at Seglarhotellet (T 5745 0400); it is open all year round and it has a great spa and restaurant (above). *www.sandhamn.com*

Bomans Hotell

Forty minutes south of Stockholm lies the quaint coastal village of Trosa where pastel-coloured wooden houses line the banks of the river and fantastic seafood restaurants, cafés and galleries are scattered around the marina. This is also where you will find the eccentric Bomans. All 44 rooms are individually decorated with items the owners have acquired over the years, mixed in with modern design pieces from Svenskt Tenn, Fritz Hansen, Philippe Starck and Ikea. We recommend you book one of the larger rooms in the band of numbers 60-75, such as Suite 60, 'La Dolce Vita', where a larger-than-life photo of Anita Ekberg bathing in Fontana di Trevi serves as a headboard.

Östra Hamnplan, Trosa, T 1565 2500, www.bomans.se

Åre
Of all Sweden's ski resorts in the north of the country, Åre (pronounced awe-re) is the most sophisticated. Come peak season (December to April) the slopes and after-ski bars and cafés are filled with the incredibly fresh-faced, healthy-looking Swedish glitterati. Stay at the luxurious Hotel Diplomat (T 06 471 7800) located in the heart of Åre. *www.are360.com*

Stallmästaregården

Stallmästaregården is so close to the centre of town that you can hardly call it an escape. But its serene setting in a park by the bay can make you feel as if you have left the city far behind you. The hotel comprises 49 charming rooms, including the large, modern, split-level suites facing the courtyard. But we recommend booking one of the smaller suites that offer captivating views of Brunnsviken bay. The restaurant dates back to the mid-1600s and is well worth a visit for its traditional cooking techniques; it even has its own smokehouse. Try the Salma smoked salmon, with white asparagus and lovage emulsion. After lunch, take a walk in nearby Haga Park and follow the path along the waterfront to the mysterious Echo Temple and Koppartälten (see p014).
Norrtull, T 610 1300,
www.stallmastaregarden.se

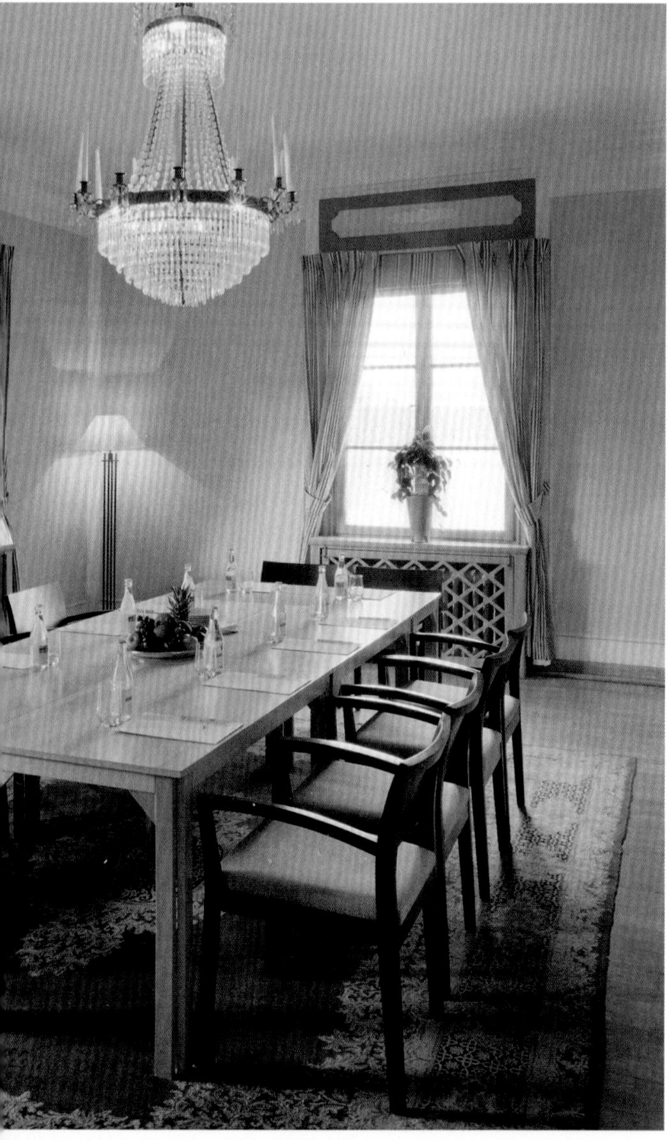

NOTES
SKETCHES AND MEMOS

RESOURCES
CITY GUIDE DIRECTORY

A

Acne 078
Norrmalmstorg 2
T 611 6411
www.acnestudios.se

Albert & Jacks 034
Skeppsbron 24
T 411 5045
www.albertjacks.com

Asplund 076
Sibyllegatan 31
T 662 5284
www.asplund.org

B

Balance 092
Lästmakargatan 10
T 407 4400
www.balancetraining.se

B Andersson Fågel & Vilt 084
Östermalms Saluhall
Östermalmstorg
T 662 5557
www.fagelvilt.se

BAR 052
Blasieholmsgatan 4a
T 611 5335
www.restaurangbar.se

Baren at Lydmar 050
Södra Blasieholmshamnen 2
T 223 160
www.lydmar.se

Byredo 074
Mäster Samuelsgatan 6
T 5250 2615
www.byredo.com

C

Caina 017
Hotel Nobis
Norrmalmstorg 2-4
T 614 1030
www.nobishotel.se

Centralbadet 088
Drottninggatan 88
T 5452 1300
www.centralbadet.se

D

Den Gyldene Freden 056
Österlånggatan 51
T 249 760
www.gyldenefreden.se

Designgalleriet 087
Odengatan 21
T 230 021
www.designgalleriet.com

Djurgårdsbrunn 033
Djurgårdsbrunnsvägen 68
T 624 2200
www.bockholmen.com/djurgardsbrunn

E

Ericsson Globe 093
Globentorget 2
T 771 310 000
www.globearenas.se

Esperanto 044
Kungstensgatan 2
T 696 2323
www.esperantorestaurant.se

F

Fifth Avenue Shoe Repair 086
Mäster Samuelsgatan 2
T 611 1640
www.shoerepair.se

HOTELS

ADDRESSES AND ROOM RATES

Berns Hotel 020
Room rates:
double, SEK1,990;
X-Large Room, from SEK3,390;
Clock Suite, SEK8,500
Näckströmsgatan 8
T 5663 2200
www.berns.se

Bomans Hotell 098
Room rates:
double room, SEK1,950;
La Dolce Vita Suite, SEK2,900
Östra Hamnplan
Trosa
T 1565 2500
www.bomans.se

Clarion Hotel 016
Room rates:
double, from SEK970
Ringvägen 98
T 462 1000
www.clarionstockholm.com

Clarion Hotel Sign 029
Room rates:
double, from SEK1,500;
Superior Room, from SEK1,300;
Suite 601, from SEK3,500
Östra Järnvägsgatan 35
T 676 9800
www.clarionsign.com

Hotel Diplomat 100
Room rates:
double, from SEK1,290
Torget Åre
T 06 471 7800
www.diplomathotel.com

Hotel Esplanade 021
Room rates:
double, SEK1,595;
Room 10, SEK,1,795;
Room 14, SEK1,795
Strandvägen 7a
T 663 0740
www.hotelesplanade.se

Gåshaga 018
Room rates:
double, SEK1,995
Värdshusvägen 14-16
Lidingö
T 601 3400
www.gashaga.nu

Grand Hôtel 028
Room rates:
double, SEK3,500;
Deluxe Room, SEK5,800;
Superior Suite, from SEK9,600;
Bernadotte Suite, SEK20,000
Södra Blasieholmshamnen 8
T 679 3500
www.grandhotel.se

Lydmar 030
Room rates:
double, from; SEK3,200;
X-Large Room, SEK12,500
Södra Blasieholmshamnen 2
T 223 160
www.lydmar.com

Hotel Nobis 017
Room rates:
double, from SEK2,790;
Tower Room, from SEK3,900;
Nobis Suite, from SEK25,000
Norrmalmstorg 2-4
T 614 1000
www.nobishotel.se

Seglarhotellet 097
Room rates:
double, SEK2,390
Riddargatan 6
T 5745 0400
www.sandhamn.com

Skeppsholmen 026
Room rates:
double, from, SEK2,300;
Room 254, from SEK3,495
Gröna Gången 1
T 440 5241
www.hotelskeppsholmen.se

Stallmästaregården 102
Room rates:
double, from SEK2,195;
Suite, from SEK4,900
Norrtull
T 610 1300
www.stallmastaregarden.se

Story Hotel 024
Room rates:
double, from SEK1,790;
Super Squeeze, SEK1,190;
Lily Dam Suite, SEK3,190
Riddargatan 6
T 5450 3940
www.storyhotels.com

WALLPAPER* CITY GUIDES

Executive Editor
Rachael Moloney

Editor
O'ar Pali
Re-edition Editor
Ella Marshall
Assistant Editor
Shanthi Sivanesan
Authors
Roberta Ellingsen Holm
Elna Nykänen Andersson

Art Director
Loran Stosskopf

Art Editor
Eriko Shimazaki
Designer
Rhian Clugston
Map Illustrator
Russell Bell

Photography Editor
Sophie Corben
**Deputy
Photography Editor**
Anika Burgess

Sub-Editor
Vanessa Harriss
Interns
Harry Fell
Tom Loader
Ella Mcleod

**Wallpaper* Group
Editor-in-Chief**
Tony Chambers
Publishing Director
Gord Ray
Managing Editor
Jessica Diamond

Contributors
Alex Bagner

Wallpaper* ® is a
registered trademark
of IPC Media Limited

First published 2006
Second edition (revised
and updated) 2010
Third edition (revised
and updated) 2011
© 2006, 2010 and 2011
IPC Media Limited

ISBN 978 0 7148 6290 3

PHAIDON

Phaidon Press Limited
Regent's Wharf
All Saints Street
London N1 9PA

Phaidon Press Inc
180 Varick Street
New York, NY 10014

Phaidon® is a registered
trademark of Phaidon
Press Limited

www.phaidon.com

A CIP Catalogue record for
this book is available from
the British Library.

Printed in China

PHOTOGRAPHERS

Marianne Boströ
Kaknästornet, p012

Felix Brüggemann
Rehns Antikhandel,
pp080-081

Johan Fowelin
Moderna Museet,
pp010-011

Peter Guenzel
Koppartälten, p014
Kulturhuset, p015
Stadsbiblioteket,
pp066-067
Asplund, p076

Yanan Li
Stadshuset,
pp070-071

Åke E:son Lindman
Matbaren, pp060-061
Gåshaga Brygga, p065

Michael McLain
Teatergrillen, p059

Peartree Digital
'Pulp' perfume, p075
'Higgins' T-shirt, p077
'Myrten' teapot, p083

Urban Orzolek
Nytorget Urban Deli, p046

Christoffer Rudquist
Stockholm City View,
inside front cover
Wenner-Gren Centre, p013
Nobis Hotel, p017
Hotel Esplanade, p021
Story Hotel, p024, p025
Clarion Hotel Sign, p029
Albert & Jacks, pp034-035
Gamla Lampor, p037
Fotografiska, p038
Restaurang AG, p041,
pp042-043
Råkultur, p047
PA&Co, p048
Frantzén/Lindeberg, p049
BAR, p052
Pontus, p053, pp054-055
Den Gyldene Freden,
p056, p057
KonstnärsBaren, p058
Camilla Modin
Djanaieff, p063
Millesgården, pp068-069
Snickarbacken 7, p073
Byredo, p074
Östermalms Saluhall,
pp084-085
Royal Lawn Tennis Club,
pp090-091
Balance, p092

Henrik Trygg
Djurgården, p033

Gabriella Wachtmeister
Gåshaga, pp018-019
Konsthantverkarna, p036
Esperanto, p044

STOCKHOLM

A COLOUR-CODED GUIDE TO THE CITY'S HOT 'HOODS

ÖSTERMALM
The chic part of Stockholm, with snazzy shopping and grand residences

SKEPPSHOLMEN
Museum Island has all the culture you could possibly need, from art to design

NORRMALM
The financial and business centre of the city with office blocks and lunch spots

SÖDERMALM
Slightly leftfield district, full of cutting-edge boutiques and boho cafés

VASASTADEN
Friendly, residential area with an emerging scene of neighbourhood eateries

GAMLA STAN
The Old Town is the tourist hub, all cobbled streets and famous buildings

KUNGSHOLMEN
Up-and-   oving in

DJURG
Urban ga   ral museums

For a full
Featured   are colour-coded, according to the district in which they are located.